DARK WEB, ACCES, CHALLENGES, REGULATIONS

VOLUME 2, ISSUE 1

KARAN YADAV

Contents

Preface

"Start writing, no matter what. The water does not flow until the faucet is turned on".

- Louis L'Amour

Hundreds of students and professors are contributing their work to Brain Booster Articles, we are here to provide ample information about Law and Contemporary issues. Our aim is to provide a platform for today's generation to express their views and ideas on law and contemporary law.

Author

CHAPTER ONE

ABSTRACT

The debate over the importance of maintaining anonymity online has become more complex due to the illegal activities that are carried out on the dark web. Policy-makers need to understand the Dark Web in order to enact effective legislation and improve the efficiency of the operations of the dark web. This paper aims to provide a comprehensive analysis of the various aspects of the dark web.

The history of the dark web continues to be relevant to the discussion about the issue of 3criminal activity on the dark web. Through the cases that have been prosecuted on the dark web, one can gain an understanding of the various policies that will be implemented in the future.

This paper aims to provide a comprehensive analysis of the various aspects of the dark web and the government's role in regulating it. It also explores the most effective and reasonable ways that the government can use to address the issue. As the US develops its policy on the dark web, other countries will be drafting regulations that will be similar to those that are already in place

CHAPTER TWO

RESEARCH QUESTION

1. Whether the current laws and legislation have regulatory affect on Dark Web
2. Parliament should consider the usage of dark web, possible crimes, parliament have to consider the existing laws which can deal with Dark Web The probable challenges that should be neutrilised in order to make it consistent for the country

RESEARCH HYPOTHESIS

1. The researcher will be test in the veracity of the following hypothesis:
2. It is assumed by the author dark web has grown , owing to which it is needed to be regulated and possible challenges to be look out

REVIEW OF THE LITERATURE

Taking of the dark webs: Law Enforcement Expert ID Talks about the challenges of regulation, in this committee was setup to critically examine the use of dark web in India and it`s challenges

Law related to Dark Web in India, in this the author points the various provision in IPC and other legislation like Information Technology Act 2005 which hints about it.

Public policy perspective of the dark web in which author the discuss the effects of dark web and it`s response

CHAPTER FIVE

INTRODUCTION

Many people have heard of the Dark Web, which is often portrayed as a place where illicit and mysterious activities are conducted. However, this misconception is not entirely accurate. The Dark Web is different from what most people think of as the internet.

The term internet refers to all the devices that are connected to a network of networks. There are two main elements of the internet: the Deep Web and the Surface Web. The Surface Web is what most people think of as the internet, as it is a collection of websites that are easily accessed through standard web browsers and internet protocols. However, this is just the tip of the iceberg as there are many more websites that are not only indexed by search engines but also come under the umbrella of other services.

The Deep Web is the vast body of information that is hidden from the users of the surface web. It is estimated that the size of this iceberg is around 5000 to 4000 times bigger than the surface web. According to researchers, the Deep Web accounts for over 90% of all traffic on the internet. This is a surprise to most people who don't realize that they are surfing this vast ocean of information regularly.

The Deep Web is considered to be the most important part of the internet as it contains data from various websites such as Facebook, Twitter, and Snapchat. These data can only be accessed through the programs that are used to access them. Other large portions of this data include files and instant messaging services such as Google Drive and Dropbox.

This paper defines the Dark Web as a small portion of the Deep Web that is inaccessible to most people. It accounts for less than 0.01 percent of the sites on the internet, and there are around 45,000 of these sites. To access these sites, users need to use a special browser known as The Onion Router or Tor.

The Dark Web is considered to be an incredibly dangerous place for people to operate due to its anonymity. It is also a sanctuary for political dissidents and cybercriminals. This paper aims to provide a better understanding of the Dark Web and how it can be monitored.

Although the term Dark Web is often used interchangeably with the Deep Web, the difference between the two is very important. The Dark Web is a distinct section of the internet that is only accessible through services such as Tor. It cannot be accessed through the surface web. The sites that are considered Dark Web must also be able to be accessed anonymously.

To be considered a Dark Web site, a website must first require a user to enter their Tor address. Some sites, on the other hand, require a password in order to protect their users. The reason why the Deep Web is not considered a part of the Dark Web is due to how it can be accessed through programs that are commonly used on the surface web.

The Dark Web has been around for a long time. The origins of the internet can be traced back to the 1960s, when the US Department of Defense started developing a network that would allow it to access its computer systems.

Although the Dark Web has been around for a long time, it became widely known in 2013 after the arrest of Ross William Ulbricht, the creator of the Silk Road.

USAGE OF DARK WEB IN INDIA

In terms of the number of people using the Dark Web, India is the biggest market. It accounts for 26% of the country's total users.

According to a report by ZDnet, a group known as the ShinyHunters tried to sell the private information of over 73 million users on the Dark Web. It breached the security of various websites, such as Social Share, Chatbooks, and Online Dating app Zoosk.

A cybersecurity firm called Cyble noted that in April 2020, around half a million zoom account were hacked. The attackers were able to sell the private information for less than one rupee.

Arxiv, a company that monitors the activities of individuals using the Dark Web, noted that 70.6% of its users are male.

The following table shows the distributive usage use of dark web in India[1]

Category Group Percentage of users using the dark web
18-25 35.9%

26-35 34.8%

36-45 16.8%

46-55 8.8%

56-65 3.1%

Above 65's 0.6%

[1]Surbhi Jindal, law student, *Dr B.R. Ambedkar National Law University, Sonipat, Haryana.*

CHAPTER SIX

MECHANISM TO ASSESS DARK WEB

To access the Dark Web, a user must first install a browser software known as Tor. Some of the other programs that are commonly used to access the Dark Web include FreeNet, TAILS, and the Onion Router. These programs allow users to navigate anonymously through the section of the internet that is only accessible through services such as Tor. Some of the other methods that are commonly used to access the Dark Web include Tunneling and Virtual Private Networks. These allow users to connect to various entities using a secure communication channel.

The popularity of Tor software has led to the number of daily users of this program reaching over two million. Unlike the browser, which is designed to allow users to hide their identities, the Tor network is different from the browser. It utilizes a layered technology known as the onion routing, which ensures that the traffic coming through its network is directed to the intended destination. This method makes the browser slower than normal connections.

During the 1990s, the US Navy's Naval Research lab developed a technology that allows it to secure communications. In 2004, it released the code for Tor, which was used by computer scientists Nick Mathewson, Roger Dingledine, and others. The group that developed the software was then known as the Tor Project. The goal of the non-profit organization was to advocate for the right to privacy and free speech.

The use of Tor has been used for various legitimate activities, such as medical communications. It can also help law enforcers track criminals and provide access to banned social media sites. Although it is not a criminal activity, intelligence agencies monitor the activities of Tor users to predict potential criminal activity.

Individuals such as Edward Snowden, who leaked information about the US government's surveillance programs, have also used TAILS software to communicate with journalists. Other methods that are commonly used to access the Dark Web include using Tor2web, which is a bridge that can be accessed using a standard browser.

CHAPTER SEVEN

EXAMPLES OF UNFAIR USE OF DARK WEB

RELATED TO CRIMINAL ACTS

The dark web is an ideal platform for criminal and terrorist activities. It allows users to conduct their activities anonymously and has a variety of features that can be used to plan and coordinate attacks. In April 2021, an Italian was arrested for hiring a hitman on the Dark Web to attack his ex-girlfriend.

In a statement, Europol noted that an Italian national used the Tor network to hire a hitman to carry out an assassination. He was able to secure the services of a hitman through an online forum known as an internet assassination site.

In 2020, a website known as Azerbaijani Eagles offered to commission a murder for $5,000. Law enforcers and experts have noted that these types of websites are usually scams. However, they noted that people are still hiring hitmen through these sites. A nurse from Illinois was sent to prison for 12 years after she used a dark web platform to hire a hitman to kill her boyfriend's wife.

Terrorist groups such as the Islamic State use the dark web to carry out their activities, such as recruiting and radicalizing individuals. The Al-Hayat Media Center, a media outlet of the ISIS, posted a link on its forum that explained how to access its website through the dark web. It also shared a message on its Telegram channel.

In March 2021, the WHO warned the public about the sale of fake Covid-19 vaccines on the dark web. These types of fraudulent products could potentially exploit the global demand for vaccines, which is currently at an all-time high. To prevent these types of activities, the organization urged the public to only use government-run vaccination programs. Besides fraudulent vaccines, other criminal activities such as drug trafficking and money laundering are also heavily linked to the dark web.

EVICT BLACKMALING

We're already talking about the illegal activities that are taking place on the dark web, and Evite was an example of this. In 2019, the social planning service experienced a security breach that affected the personal information of over 10 million of its users.

Due to the importance of its users' privacy, Evite has taken various steps to ensure that its platform is secure. One of these is implementing a comprehensive security measure that prevents unauthorized access and use of its platform.

The hacker who triggered the security breach was identified as Gnosticplayers. Although he didn't release any information about the incident to the public, he asked for $1900 in Bitcoin in order to settle the dispute. This is a relatively small amount of money, as data breaches can cost companies a lot of money in settlements.

Evite refused to pay, and the hacker was able to access and sell the company's data on the dark web. The market where he was selling the data was then shut down. Ever since the incident occurred, there has been no sign of any developments regarding the situation. The selling and stealing of private information on the dark web is always very distressing for the victims.

This incident is the only data theft-related story that we're currently talking about. Due to the increasing number of police show cases, we're also starting to see more cases of data theft.

THE HITMAN CRIMES

The dark web is known for its numerous hitmen for hire sites. Due to the image of the platform, many people have started to believe that they can have their loved one killed using Bitcoin.

There are a lot of stories about individuals getting their problems resolved by hiring hitmen on the dark web. However, before you can hire a hitman, you need to thoroughly research the services available on the dark web.

A Reddit story posted by a user who claimed to have hired a hitman for fun has gained a lot of attention. Despite the captivating nature of the story, it's not surprising that these services would be operating on the dark web.

If you're worried that the details about this scheme might seem a bit shady, The New York Times has a story for you. They found that the services involved in this scam would typically take the money from the buyers, and then they would never deliver.

DATA BREACHES IN INDIA

In January 2021, a security breach at Juspay exposed the data of over 10 million customers. The data included various details such as mobile numbers and email IDs.

In March 2021, the data of over 3.5 million users of the mobile wallet company was also available for sale on the dark web. The details of these users, which included their contact details and their Aadhar card details, were stolen. The Reserve Bank of India then ordered a forensic audit of the company.

In April 2021, Domino's India suffered a security breach that exposed the details of over 18 crore orders. According to Alon Gal, the CTO of Hudson Rock, the data was sold on the dark web for around Rs 4.5 crore.

In April 2021, the data of BigBasket's customers was allegedly stolen and sold on the dark web. The database included the names, birth dates, and email addresses of over 20 million customers. The data was allegedly sold by a hacker group known as the ShinyHunters. The group was able to access the database in a size of around 3.25 GB.

CHAPTER EIGHT

REGULATORY CHALLENEGES

Due to the nature of the dark web's anonymity and encryption technique, it's difficult for law enforcers and policymakers to monitor its activities. This means that they're not able to collect enough information to combat cybercrimes.

The lack of a clear definition of cyber terrorism has made it difficult for intelligence agencies to determine which activities are related to the crime. Cyberspace is a multi-dimensional threat that can be influenced by multiple factors.

Besides strong encryption techniques, the majority of the financial transactions that are conducted on the dark web are conducted in cryptocurrencies. These types of transactions provide a level of anonymity that's not available with other forms of transactions. The underlying technology of these cryptocurrencies is known as the block chain.

The nature of the data that's stored on the dark web makes it incredibly difficult to access and modify. For instance, the group responsible for the attack on the Colonial Pipeline demanded a ransom of $5 million in cryptocurrencies. The REvil gang, which targeted hundreds of businesses in early 2021, also demanded a ransom of bitcoin.

Due to the nature of the transactions that are conducted on the dark web, it's incredibly difficult for law enforcers to monitor the activities of criminal organizations. Since cryptocurrencies are commonly used for illegitimate purposes, their regulation is only possible if they're used for their legitimate purposes.

One of the most challenging factors when it comes to monitoring the activities of criminal organizations is the classification of all the roles involved in the financial transactions. Currently, block chain technology is still in its infancy and requires more expertise to develop. Another issue with the dark web is that most of its sites stay active for up to 200 days. It's incredibly tedious to track these types of transactions, as some of them only last for a couple of months.

GENERAL CHALLENGES

Despite the increasing number of criminal organizations using the dark web, law enforcers still lack the necessary data to effectively monitor its activities.

Dark web activity crosses national and local borders. Because of this, investigators need to work together with law enforcers from other agencies in order to combat the activities of criminal organizations on the dark web. According to experts, if authorities don't enforce laws against illegal activities on the dark web, criminal organizations will be more inclined to conduct illicit business.

Some law enforcers are worried that they might be exposed to retaliation from the malicious users of the dark web. This is why it's important that they understand the nature of the dark web and how it can be used to fight crime. Despite the lack of data on the dark web, it's still important that law enforcers have the necessary tools and resources to effectively monitor its activities.

Participants suggested that trainers should talk about the similarities and differences between traditional investigations and the investigations carried out on the dark web.

They suggested that command buy-in sessions be conducted to encourage law enforcers to start investigating and training on the dark web. These sessions could be very beneficial for the funding of the investigations and training.

For specialized units, such as those focused on evidence preservation, these sessions should also be conducted to introduce the concepts of the dark web.

Participants also identified the training needs of various units, such as those focused on evidence preservation. They noted that the training needs of these units were more than other areas.

TECHINAL CHALLENGES

Despite the anonymity of the dark web, basic tools can still be used by people who are motivated to conduct illicit activities. According to a report by the RAND Corporation, people can easily start using the dark web without much difficulty. Law enforcers can sometimes compromise the information of buyers and sellers on the dark web due to the de-anonymization of their transactions. However, users have developed additional tools to protect their data.

One of the biggest challenges that law enforcers face when it comes to interdicting dark web shipments is the amount of parcels that they have to deal with. The US Postal Service is estimated to move over 500 million parcels a day.

During the workshop, the experts identified the need for research regarding the various laws that apply to searching packages.

IDENTIFICATION

They also discussed the need for line officers to develop a better understanding of the scope and types of illicit transactions that they can encounter on the dark web. Participants noted that the creation of task forces could help law enforcers share information.

PROTECTION RELATED TO PRIVICY OF INDIVISUAL

Participants also discussed the need for federal agencies to provide guidance on how to manage the privacy concerns that individuals have when it comes to participating in investigations. Although they were not identified as a priority, they noted the need for research on how much individuals would sacrifice in order to protect their personal information.

IDENTIFICATION OF THE SUSPECT

According to the participants, law enforcers need to develop the ability to identify items that could be used by suspects to access the dark web.

EVIDENCE IDENTIFICATION, ACCESS, PRESERVATION

The challenge of gathering and preserving technical data has become more challenging for law enforcers as they try to make evidence that can be used by juries to determine the guilt or innocence of individuals accused of using the dark web. Due to the increasing number of data formats and the complexity of the investigations, cross-jurisdictional coordination is also needed.

Due to the nature of the anonymity and encryption features of the dark web, the participants noted the need for law enforcers to use best practices when it comes to gathering evidence. One of the most important factors that the experts identified during the workshop was the establishment of standards for the processes that they can use to collect evidence from the dark web.

The success of law enforcers in disrupting criminal activities on the dark web often leads to the emergence of new markets and the quickening of the users' adaptation to the new environment. During the workshop, the participants noted that there are also exchanges between users on how to avoid detection.

NEEDS

The complexity of the criminal activities that are carried out on the dark web and the varying laws that apply to it have made it more challenging for law enforcers to effectively address the issue.

Participants also discussed the potential risks that law enforcers could face when they interact with individuals who are using the dark web. One of the issues that they noted was the possibility of entrapment, which occurs when authorities use fake identities to establish trust with criminals.

CHAPTER TEN

CONCLUSION

Law enforcement authorities identified priority needs for investigating criminal activity on the dark web:

- Raising awareness of the dark web among state and local authorities.
- Forging cross-jurisdictional partnerships among agencies.
- Initiating more and better training to equip officers to identify dark web evidence and activity.
- Equipping special investigation units with advanced knowledge of dark web methods and activities. Because of the clandestine nature of the dark web, many state and local law enforcement agencies are generally unaware of its existence and its capacity for engendering crime in their jurisdictions.[1]

[1]NIJ REPORT PUBLISHED ON 15TH JUNE 2015